Wright Middle

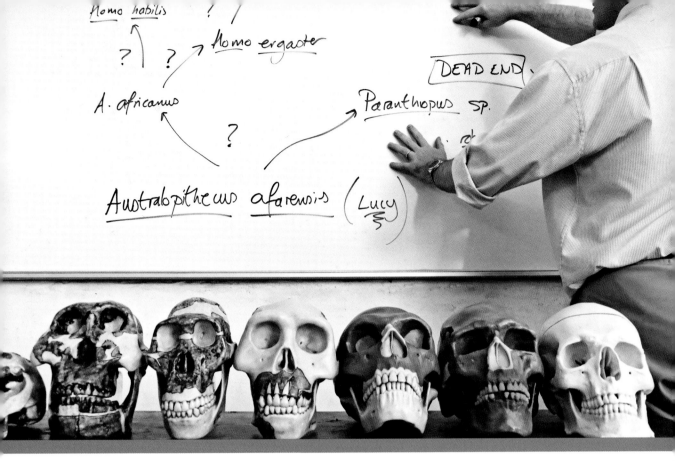

Evolution

Homo habilis ! ?

? | ? → Homo ergaster

A. africanus

?

→ Paranthrop

Australopithecus afarensis (Lucy)

DEBATING
THE ISSUES

Evolution

DANIEL
ARDIA
AND
ELIZABETH
RICE

Cavendish
Square

New York

Homo habilis ? ?

→ *Homo ergaster*

Library of Congress Cataloging-in-Publication Data

Ardia, Daniel.
Evolution / by Daniel Ardia and Elizabeth Rice.
  p. cm. — (Debating the issues)
Includes index.
ISBN 978-1-62712-410-2 (hardcover) ISBN 978-1-62712-411-9 (paperback) ISBN 978-1-62712-412-6 (ebook)
1. Evolution (Biology) — Juvenile literature. I. Ardia, Daniel. II. Title.
QH367.1 A73 2014
576—dc23

Editor: Peter Mavrikis
Art Director: Anahid Hamparian
Series design by Sonia Chaghatzbanian
Production Manager: Jennifer Ryder-Talbot
Production Editor: Andrew Coddington

Photo research by Alison Morretta

Australopithecus afarensis

Table of Contents

Chapter 1

For as long as humans have lived, they have been keen observers of the natural world. The earliest peoples lived close to nature because they hunted animals, fished, and foraged for food. Our earliest ideas about groups of organisms, what are now called **species**, were that they had come into being as they were and had never changed. Over two thousand years ago, the ancient Greeks were the first Western thinkers to attempt to explain where plants and animals came from. According to their writings, they believed that plants and animals came from the generative power of nature rather than through the purposeful creation of a god. A common thread in the ideas of the ancient Greeks was that plants and animals were unchangeable. In other words, the way they look now is identical to the way they looked when they first appeared on the earth. The philosopher Plato believed that nature could not change because the world is an interconnected whole that lives in harmony. If plants and animals changed, this harmony would be disrupted.

The ideas of the ancient Greeks had a very strong influence on the way that later philosophers and scientists viewed and understood the origin of plants and animals. It is not surprising that over the course of

Humans have always been curious about the natural world. Over time curiosity combined with reason and observations has given us our modern understanding of how the world works.

time, many of the ideas of the ancient Greeks were discovered to be wrong. Having no way to determine how old the world was, they did not imagine that living things had existed on the earth for as long as modern geologists now believe they did.

Changing Views

To best understand modern views on species and evolution, it is help-ful to consider how ideas have themselves evolved and changed over time. About three hundred years ago began an intellectual and scien-tific movement called the **Enlightenment**. During its early stages, the understanding of life was dominated by two ideas:

(1) Species were unchanged and the product of special creation. "Special creation" meant that a particular species was created in its current form and had not changed in appearance or habits since it first appeared on the earth.

(2) The earth was "young"—only about six thousand years old.

Enlightenment thinkers made important discoveries that challenged those beliefs and set the foundation for the modern understanding of life.

The Classification System

Living organisms are typically known by their common name: African elephant, Bengal tiger, boa constrictor, monarch butterfly. However,

Linnaeus's System of Classification

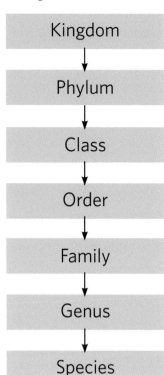

Linnaeus's system of classification gave scientists a common language to name organisms and works to this day because it is hierarchical so that each species is nested within the larger groupings above it.

because the world has so many languages, it is very important that every species has a scientific name, that way scientists from all over the world know that they are talking about the same species. A classification system is important because it allows **naturalists** to categorize living creatures. Once plants and animals are in categories, scientists have the foundation to conduct research about how they are related.

The Discovery of Extinction

Now having a system with which to describe and categorize nature, scientists could apply these techniques to **fossils**, preserved remains of plants and animals. It became clear that there was strong evidence that species of animals and plants have disappeared, or become extinct, over time. In the 1700s and 1800s English and French scientists described and classified fossils of species for which no living examples had been found. Dinosaurs are the most well known example of an extinct species, but scientists have studied thousands of fossils of other animals and plants that have also disappeared. The presence of extinct species was important to developing ideas about evolution because if species had been created through special creation, then why would they have become extinct? As scientists looked at the fossils, it was obvious to them that living species shared many similarities with extinct species. This pattern was a puzzle because each species, living or extinct, was believed to represent a unique creation event; so there was no reason to expect or predict that living organisms would share similarities with and thus likely be related to any extinct species. A particularly interesting pattern was noted by the French naturalist Georges Cuvier (1768–1832). He observed that the lower (and thus older) a geologic layer, the more different the organisms are from modern species.

Extending the Age of the Earth

The last building block that set the stage for the debate on evolution was the work by geologists that extended the estimate of the age of the earth

The famous fossil Archaeopteryx is considered by evolutionary biologists an organism at the transition between birds and their reptilian ancestors.

from six thousand years to millions of years. William Smith (1769–1839), an English geologist, mineralogist, and surveyor, described how different geological formations had distinct and predictable animal and plant fossils. The most important early geologist was a Scotsman named James Hutton (1726–1797). Hutton spent his life observing geologic activity, and he concluded that the surface of the earth is being perpetually formed and reformed. For example, lava and other molten material make mountains. The mountains then slowly erode through the action of water and chemicals and form sediments and sand, which wash away; mountains again are reformed by new lava. His critical leap in understanding led him to hypothesize that the history of the earth could be determined by understanding processes occurring in the present, as he believed that erosion and the buildup of sediments occurred similarly at any point in time. On the basis of how slowly erosion occurs, Hutton estimated the age of the earth as being millions of years old.

Following on Hutton's discoveries, Charles Lyell (1797–1875) made an important philosophical contribution to modern science. He took Hutton's idea about using the present to understand the past and applied it broadly to begin to explain how to scientifically study change in nature. In a series of influential books, he described his idea that gradual change over very long time periods is constantly occurring and that to understand that change it is necessary to study current change. Lyell was the first to hypothesize that entirely natural processes could

The wavy patterns in these rock layers on the island of Fuerteventura were evidence to early geologists that powerful forces such as volcanoes were constantly changing the surface or interior of the earth.

be used to study and explain the earth's geological patterns. Before Lyell, it was common to evoke supernatural causes in a scientific context. Lyell's arguments were so convincing to the majority of geologists and naturalists that supernatural explanations for patterns in nature became more and more scarce. Lyell and most other scientists of his time were deeply religious men. However, they found that natural processes were sufficient to describe and explain patterns in nature without having to evoke supernatural explanations.

Charles Darwin

In 1831, a young English naturalist named Charles Darwin (1809–1882) set out on a long sea voyage with a copy of Lyell's book. The voyage was expected to last only two years. Instead it took five years. At the time Darwin left England on his voyage, the question of species and whether they could change was of great interest. There were many patterns and puzzles that scientists considering this question could not solve. Extinction raised the question of why species were created that then disappeared from the earth. Other facts had emerged that also required an explanation. For example, over the previous century voyages of exploration and discovery had made obvious to Europeans that the diversity of life was much grander than they had expected. The fact that species were distributed almost randomly across the world raised many questions. Another big problem was the presence of structures that appear to have no function, as this was contradictory to the belief that species had been created to fit their environments.

THE VOYAGE OF THE BEAGLE

Darwin's five-year trip around the world changed his life and changed the world. Darwin was not an official crew member on the journey. Instead he was invited by the ship's captain, Robert FitzRoy, to be a geologist (which is what Darwin thought of himself as). FitzRoy wanted to have a gentleman companion on board to eat meals with. Darwin had intended to settle down as a country parson (Anglican priest), but he decided to take the trip first. The objective of the voyage was to make nautical maps, mostly of southern South America. This was slow tedious work; so the *Beagle* would often leave Darwin on land for long periods. It is estimated that he spent more of his time on land than on the ship. And for this he was lucky. Darwin was seasick during much of his time on board, but he still managed to spend five years crossing the globe. Darwin shared a very small cabin with another crew member and they had to clear everything off their small table so that Darwin could hang his hammock to sleep. When the trip was over and Darwin returned home, he never left Great Britain again.

Darwin's voyage on the Beagle covered the globe and lasted five years even though Darwin thought he would be home within two years.

Darwin's voyage allowed him to observe a wide range of land and sea environments and habitats. During his voyage, Darwin made a number of observations that helped him formulate his theories.

For one, he found fossils of distinct extinct species in locations where species that closely resembled the fossils lived. For example,

The fossil on the left is a reconstruction of the giant ground sloth *Megatherium americanum* found in the same locations as the modern three-toed sloth shown on the right. Darwin observed both fossil sloth specimens and living three-toed sloths during his voyage.

living species of sloths are found only in locations where fossils of the extinct giant ground sloth are found. He did not think it was a coincidence that the living species tended to be found in locations where there were fossils that resembled them. He later hypothesized that the living species were related to the extinct species and that the resemblance was due to shared ancestry.

Also, as Darwin journeyed through the tropics, he was particularly struck by how well adapted species were to their environments. Plants and their **pollinators** were of particular interest to Darwin. For example, many orchids have long, complicated flowers that can be pollinated only by hummingbird species with a specially shaped bill. He concluded that species of orchids and their pollinators evolved together slowly and that changes in the flowers led to changes in the bill of the birds.

DID YOU KNOW?

Early naturalists puzzled over why large, flightless birds that lived far apart such as ostriches (Africa), rheas (South America), and emus (Australia) could be so similar to each other. Later, geologists discovered that the earth's crust floats and can move across the earth's surface. The evolutionary relationships among flightless birds became clear as the group started before the earth's land mass split into continents.

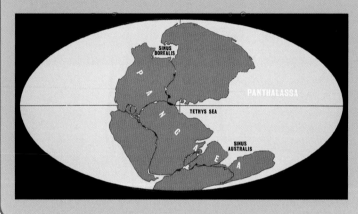

A drawing of the position of the continents about 200 million years ago showing one huge supercontinent prior to the geologic forces known as plate tectonics moving each plate to their current location.

Finally, islands provided a special window of insight for Darwin. Islands, because of their isolation, tend to contain many unique species; however, those species consistently most closely resemble species on the nearest mainland. In other words, island species tend to share many characteristics with the closest possible source of colonizing species. Darwin described a phenomenon that is now called adaptive radiation. It occurs when related species on an island show a wide range of differences in shape and size but still have a number of important similarities. Darwin's finches are a good example. Darwin's finches are a group of fourteen species that live on the Galápagos Islands off the

This remarkable photo is of the Morgan's sphinx moth, which has a 12" tongue. Darwin predicted that such a moth would exist after seeing orchids with flowers 12" deep; the moth was discovered in 1903.

coast of Ecuador. Each species has a distinct bill type; some have short, stout bills, and others have long narrow bills. However, even though they tend to differ so much in appearance (Darwin and others misclassified some species as other bird groups), they share a core set of **traits**.

Darwin's observations of the close resemblance between extinct and living species and the strong resemblance of island species to nearby mainland species require no special explanation if a creator intended to create them that way. However, Darwin, who was influenced by Lyell, explained these patterns as natural, observable processes. So, the best explanation he could provide was that of

17

shared ancestry. In other words, modern sloths shared many traits with extinct sloths because they had inherited them from the same ancestral species. As the environment changed and exerted pressures on each species, they changed in different ways until they became two different species.

Darwin did not have a eureka moment during his voyage. Rather, his ideas developed over time. After his return to England, he settled into a country house outside London and spent the rest of his life conducting experiments and working on what he called "the species question." While traveling, he had sent the specimens he collected back to England. He settled into identifying and classifying these hundreds of plant and animal species.

Darwin's writings reveal that he began to develop new ideas about life. During the twenty-odd years between returning from his voyage and the publication of his book *On the Origin of Species*, his thinking reflected the following four main influences.

Darwin's Finches

In particular, Darwin was inspired by the birds he collected in the Galápagos Islands. The birds now known as Darwin's finches were variously classified as one of several unrelated bird species, including a woodpecker and a warbler, in addition to a number of different finches. However, an **ornithological** expert who examined the birds concluded that, while they differed greatly in bill size and shape, they were all finches. In other words, they all shared distinct characteristics

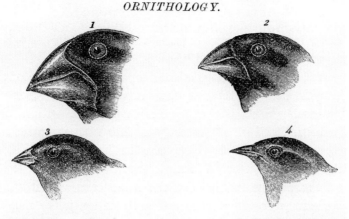

ORNITHOLOGY.

1. Geospiza magnirostris.
3. Geospiza parvula.
2. Geospiza fortis.
4. Certhidea olivacea.

This plate from an early natural history book shows four species of "Darwin's finches" from the Galápagos Islands; each differs in bill shape but all share a common finch ancestor.

that are found only in finches. Darwin was not only greatly surprised, he also realized that he had neglected to record from which island he had collected each species. Eventually, by examining specimens collected by other crew members of the *Beagle*, Darwin was able to determine where each species was found.

Two critical **hypotheses** emerged from the pattern of so many species of birds that all shared finch characteristics but differed so much in bill shape and size, as well as in behavior. The first hypothesis was that all of the species shared a single common ancestor, a finch species that had colonized the Galápagos Islands in the past. The second hypothesis related to how this single founding finch species was modified over time to give rise to the wide diversity found in the fourteen species

DID YOU KNOW?

It is now known that the closest relative of Darwin's Galápagos finches is a small finch called the grassquit, found in South America.

of modern finches. Darwin proposed a theory of **natural selection** as the cause of this modification of a common ancestor.

Thomas Malthus

The second important influence on Darwin was an English economist named Thomas Malthus. Malthus was particularly interested in human population change. He first made the mathematical observation that human populations have the capacity to grow at very high rate because each female born will eventually grow up to have children of her own. However, most populations do not grow at the maximum rate that they could. Malthus observed that disease and famine played a large part in keeping populations in check. Darwin took Malthus's ideas and applied them to the natural world. He saw how a struggle for existence occurs as individuals compete for scarce and finite resources such as food, shelter, water, and mates. One of Darwin's insightful proposals was that individuals more effective at competing are the ones that tend to leave more offspring for the next generation.

Artificial Selection

Darwin combined these two ideas—common ancestry of species and the effective struggle for existence—into his next twenty years of study. He focused on how characteristics might be passed from one generation to another. An important source of insight into the capacity of plants and animals to change comes from plant and animal breeding, what is now called **artificial selection**. For ten thousand years, people have chosen to replant seeds from plants with the sweetest, biggest, brightest fruits. The selection pressure that transformed corn from a cereal grass into corn on the cob was not natural selection but instead human-driven artificial selection. Darwin spent much of his time talking with farmers and plant and animal breeders to discover how well characteristics are passed on from parent to offspring. For example, dairy cows vary in how much milk they can produce. When farmers select only the top milk-producing females to have calves, the average milk production of the herd goes up. Their choice reflects an understanding of the fact that individuals vary in their ability to survive and reproduce. The composition of a population will change over time, depending on which individuals survive and successfully reproduce.

Darwin's observations and experiments led him to apply the idea of artificial selection to the natural world. He used logic to conclude that if

(1) there is a struggle for existence; and
(2) individuals differ in their abilities in the struggle; and
(3) those differences in abilities are passed on in part to offspring; then logically
(4) the makeup of a population will change over time.

The percent of individuals who possess features that allow them to survive and reproduce in their environment will thus increase. Darwin termed this change in the population natural selection.

Natural Selection

Darwin is also remembered for the idea of **descent with modification**. Individuals inherit characteristics from their ancestors, and those characteristics may reflect both close relatives as well as those from the distant past (descent). However, individuals are not a perfect copy of their parents, and as struggle for existence leads to different individuals surviving and reproducing, groups of individuals change over time (modification through natural selection).

Because Darwin knew that his contemporaries and especially his deeply religious wife Emma would be troubled by the implications of his ideas, he intended to have his findings published after he died. His world changed one day in 1858, however, when he received a letter from a young naturalist named Alfred Russel Wallace. Wallace had been living in the Indonesian archipelago for many years gathering animal and plant specimens for collectors back in Europe. In his letter, Wallace outlined views very similar to Darwin's. Even though he had spent fourteen years recording his ideas in his journals, Darwin was willing to let Wallace take the credit for fear of being accused of stealing Wallace's insight. Thanks to Darwin's friends Joseph Hooker and Charles Lyell, the papers of both naturalists were read at a meeting of a scientific society, and they received joint credit. In 1859, Darwin wrote a longer explanation of his thoughts on descent with modification and natural selection, titled *On the Origin of Species by Means of Natural Selection*, which was published the same year.

The reaction to Darwin's book prompted controversy. Most people rejected the idea of natural selection, often because they misunderstood Darwin's argument. As discussed earlier, the main idea at the time was that every species had been created separately. Darwin's claim that two species had shared an ancestor was difficult for people to believe. Even though the discussions across Europe and the United States became heated, scientists slowly came to accept Darwin's ideas about how life evolved. By the time Darwin died in 1882, most biologists were comfortable with the idea that species had changed over time. How this occurred was a matter for future debates.

WHAT DO YOU THINK?

How important is the age of the earth to Darwin's idea of gradual change over time?

Why don't scientists invoke the supernatural in explaining nature? How would it affect science if it was more common to explain nature using a creator?

What are the costs and benefits of offspring not looking exactly like their parents?

What kinds of features of pets and farm animals do you think are different from their wild relatives and can be best explained by artificial selection?

If you were Darwin, would you have waited to publish your book until after your death?

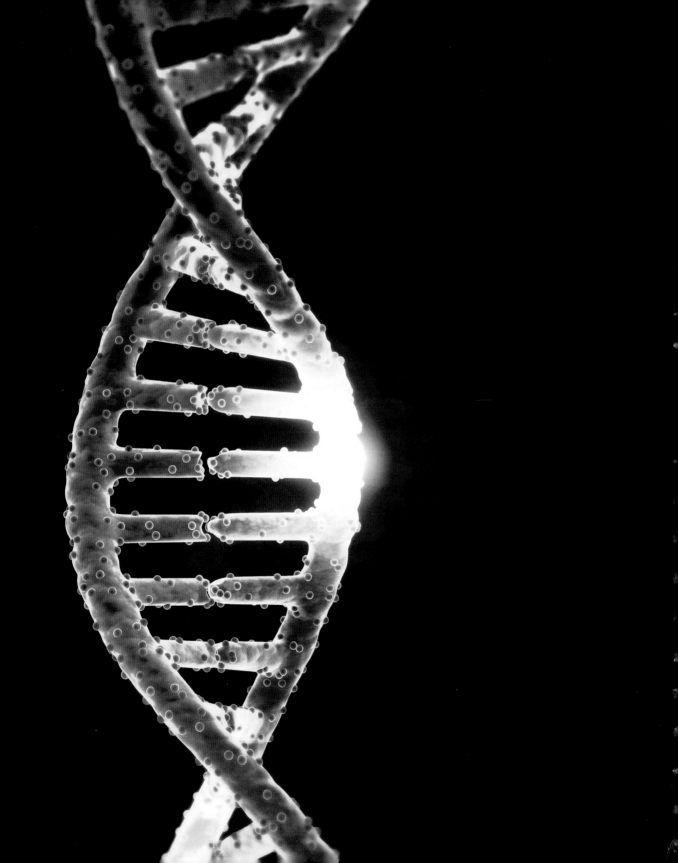

Chapter 2

Nothing in biology makes sense except in light of evolution.

—THEODOSIUS DOBZHANSKY, GENETICIST

What Is Evolution?

What evidence is there to support the idea that organisms have evolved over time from common ancestors? To investigate this question, we should first identify the possible explanations for the observations of the plants and animals on the earth. One explanation is separate creation: the idea that organisms originated separately and have not changed over time. The other is evolution: the idea that all organisms share a common ancestor. Since Darwin defined evolution as "descent with modification," we can further refine our prediction. Descent refers to the shared evolutionary history of organisms and the inheritance of genetic information, called deoxyribonucleic acid (**DNA**), from ancestors. Modification refers to how and why populations and thus species change over time. Thus, the basis for evolutionary arguments will be facts and observations that reveal (1) shared characteristics that show common ancestry among living organisms and (2) evidence of how those features have been modified to give rise to modern life.

An artist's image showing the characteristic helix shape of DNA.

Evidence of a Common Ancestry: Anatomical Features

Do living species share common features that can be best explained by shared ancestry? In other words, do two species have similar features because they inherited those features from the same common ancestor species at some point in the past? It is important to distinguish between similar traits that occur because of shared pressures of life and those that cannot be explained by shared lifestyles. For example, the wings of birds and bats likely are similar because of the benefits of catching flying prey, not because the most recent common ancestor of birds and bats had wings. Scientists look for examples of shared features that cannot be explained by shared lifestyles.

A striking example of shared features because of inheritance from a common ancestor is the structure of the limbs of tetrapods, the group of animals that includes amphibians, reptiles, birds, and mammals. All the members of these groups have five digits at the end of their limbs and other identical arrangements of the bones that make up the limbs. Yet the flippers on a penguin, the hind legs of a frog, and the front legs of a horse have very different functions and shapes. The fact that these organisms that look different and live in different environments all share limbs with identical features can be explained by inheritance from a common ancestor. Particularly convincing to some scientists is the presence of structures that are associated with hind limbs in whales even though whales do not have hind limbs. These structures are **vestigial**; that is, they have no apparent function but resemble structures

Homologies of the forelimb in six vertebrates

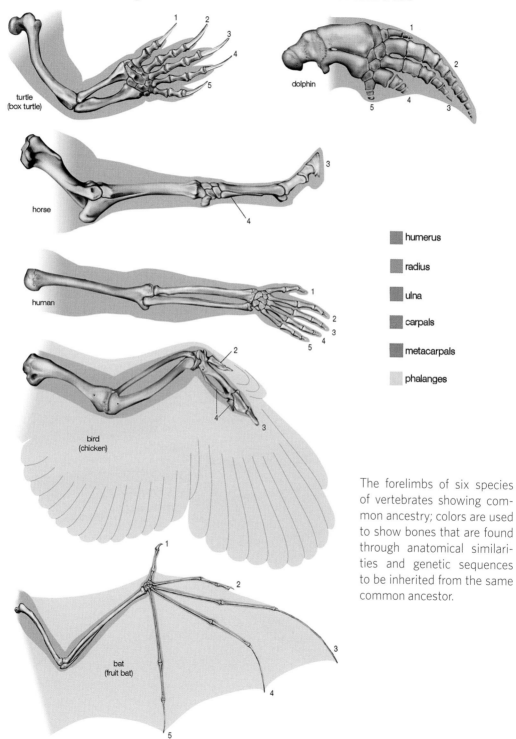

turtle (box turtle)

dolphin

horse

human

bird (chicken)

bat (fruit bat)

- humerus
- radius
- ulna
- carpals
- metacarpals
- phalanges

The forelimbs of six species of vertebrates showing common ancestry; colors are used to show bones that are found through anatomical similarities and genetic sequences to be inherited from the same common ancestor.

found in ancestors. The presence of vestigial structures is best explained as having been inherited from a previous ancestor rather than as coming from separate creation.

Further evidence of shared ancestry is found in the embryos of **vertebrates**, the group that includes tetrapods and fish. All the early stages of these organisms, including humans, show identical features, such as pouches in the throat, that eventually develop to become different

On its hind flipper, the Northern Fur Seal has toenails considered vestigial because the hind flipper is constantly in water and not used for grooming.

HOW TO MAKE A FLY AND A PERSON

A new field of biology has emerged in the last twenty years that has shown us how much all animals share in common. The field is called evolutionary developmental biology, or "evo-devo" for short. One discovery is that important genes called hox genes control where, when, and for how long the genes that build bodies are turned on. Even though flies and humans look so different from each other, it turns out that they both share very similar hox genes. The genes are not identical but are similar enough to indicate that humans and flies both inherited them from a common ancestor. One way that animals became more complex was when these genes were "mistakenly" duplicated during reproduction. One copy stayed the same and kept making the same body part. The other changed through mutation and was able to produce a new body part. Over time new additions allowed organisms to become more and more complex. For example, repeating segments of simpler organisms like millipedes evolved to be specialized structures such as the claws and antenna of lobsters. The body parts such as organs and limbs of mammals can be explained in the same way.

features in the adults of each group. If organisms were created separately, it would be logical to assume that they would not share so many similar features. This high degree of similarity in features that are not part of the function of an organism in its natural environment can be best explained by sharing a common ancestor.

Evidence of a Common Ancestry: Genetic Features

During Darwin's time and into the early 1900s, understanding and demonstrating evolution was difficult because of a lack of understanding of how characteristics were inherited. This was before the discovery of DNA, the substance that encodes genetic information. Once scientists

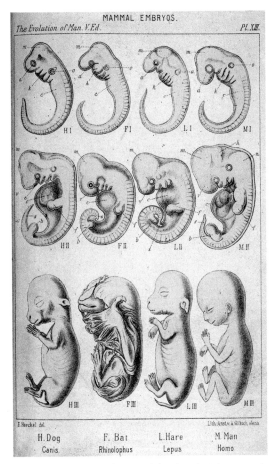

H I   F I   L I   M I

H II   F II   L II   M II

H III   F III   L III   M III

E. Haeckel del.   Lith.Anst.v.A.Giltsch, Jena.

H. Dog	F. Bat	L. Hare	M. Man
Canis.	Rhinolophus	Lepus	Homo

Drawings of the embryos of the dog, bat, hare, and man showing strong similarities in appearance early in development (top images) and gradually developing into body plans characteristics of their current body shapes.

discovered genetics, testing the predictions that Darwin made in his writings became possible. If species were created separately through creation, then we would not predict any shared genetic material among organisms. However, if species all share a common ancestor, then widespread similarities in genetic material would be expected. These similarities would indicate that all living species inherited genetic information from a common ancestor.

The evidence for shared genetic features is overwhelming. All living organisms utilize the same underlying genetic code: DNA. Using similar cellular machinery, all organisms read DNA in sets of three bases in order to decode genetic information into proteins. This is very strong evidence that the oldest common ancestor of living things utilized this same three-section code. Therefore, we all share it in common because we all evolved from that long-ago species.

This shared genetic code, along with the anatomical similarities, is strong evidence of shared ancestry that does not require evidence of long-term change, a common criticism of evolution. Rather, by simple

DID YOU KNOW?

In 1934, an American bacteriologist named Oswald Avery proposed that DNA might contain genetic information. His scientific colleagues found the idea absurd. At the time, scientists knew that genetic information came from chromosomes. Chromosomes are composed of proteins and DNA. Proteins are complex and diverse. DNA is composed of only four bases. Therefore, scientists reasoned that the complex proteins must be the source of genetic information. His scientific colleagues believed that DNA, with only four bases, could not possibly encode all the rich information needed to form an individual. Twenty more years passed before scientists established that how DNA was read, which allowed geneticists to decode the genetic information.

logic and probability, the only likely explanation for why all organisms share similar features is that they have evolved from a common ancestor. Thus, the pattern of shared specific features that have no direct link to how organisms function is more consistent with the hypothesis of descent with modification (evolution) than with the hypothesis of separate creation.

Genetics offers insights into different periods of time in evolutionary history. For example, scientists interested in comparing the salmon from different rivers can look for small changes in parts of DNA that do not produce proteins. (The parts that do produce proteins change much more slowly because they are more important for survival—and therefore under much pressure from natural selection.) Sometimes, simply by chance, a change—or **mutation**—occurs in DNA. As mutations are rare, each individual has a few small differences in its DNA compared to a recent ancestor. Two fish that share the same rare differences are likely to have shared a common ancestor more recently than individuals or species that do not share the same rare mutations. The same approach can be applied to estimating how long ago two relatively unrelated species shared a common ancestor. Scientists can estimate the rate at which mutations build up in DNA and use this rate as a clock. So, by comparing how different two species are and estimating the amount of time necessary for genetic differences to occur, it is possible to estimate how long ago two species shared a common ancestor.

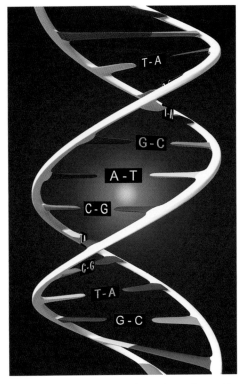

All living organisms use the universal genetic code, the same four letter base sequence that leads to the same amino acids during the process of creating proteins from DNA.

Evidence from Fossils

Fossils are the preserved remains of previously living organisms. Fossils often formed when organisms were covered with sediment. Over time and under pressure, the biological materials changed to become minerals, which were preserved in hard rock. Because fossils are rare, there is only a small snapshot of previous life to examine. The lack of evidence for particular moments in life's history is not evidence that evolution did or did not occur. We can only examine the evidence we have, although new fossils are found every year.

DID YOU KNOW?

Because salmon return to their river of birth to reproduce, salmon from two nearby rivers rarely share genes. The salmon in each river are isolated from each other and have different genetic makeup. To help protect and manage the fish, fisheries biologists term each population an evolutionary significant unit.

Fossil evidence supports the hypothesis of evolution (descent with modification) and does not support the hypothesis that species were created separately. For example, recently discovered fossils of a four-legged animal that lived in water are believed to represent the transition between hoofed land-dwelling animals and modern whales and dolphins. This remarkable creature had features indicating it spent most of the time in the water and had begun evolving features similar to those of whales. However, it still retained hooves and other features of land-dwelling mammals. This transitional fossil is consistent with the genetic similarities between modern whales and modern hoofed animals. They share more genetic material in common than they do with other mammals. Combined with the fossil evidence, this genetic similarity provides two independent lines of evidence that whales and hoofed mammals evolved from a common ancestor.

Some kinds of animals are more likely to form fossils and be preserved more than others. For example, hard-shelled marine organisms such as clams are commonly preserved in marine rocks. By examining the shell shape and size of clams over long periods of geologic time, scientists have demonstrated clearly that clam species did not stay the

While the fossil records have biases in the kinds of organisms that are preserved, the similarities between fossils and living organisms are used as evidence of change over time and shared ancestry among life.

same over time but rather changed in appearance. One striking pattern is that clam fossils showing rapid changes in appearance are from geologic times with drastic environmental change. This link between evolutionary change and environmental change is consistent with the idea that species are modified over time.

Evidence from Experimental Studies of Natural Selection

In science, the most conclusive evidence comes from experiments. Because experiments involve manipulating conditions, it is possible to isolate all other factors to find out if the predicted influence is responsible. One reason biologists have such confidence in the theory of evolution is that thousands of experiments have shown consistent support for common descent and the important role of natural selection.

The best examples of studies showing evolution in the laboratory are done with bacteria. Bacteria grow quickly; so it is possible to grow many generations and observe the composition of the population change over time. A common approach is to subject identical groups of bacteria to an environmental stress, such as temperature change or limited food supply, and then allow them to grow for many generations.

Because a small number of individuals will have the best features to survive under the experimental conditions, they will grow at faster rates and increase in abundance compared with the other individuals. This success will lead to evolutionary change through natural selection—the population will change over time, diverging from the original population but still retaining some original characteristics. In other words, it will show descent with modification.

Rigorous experimental research demonstrating natural selection and evolution does not occur just in the laboratory. Scientists working on the Caribbean island of Trinidad have been studying a species of fish, a guppy that lives in pools of streams running down mountains of the tropical rain forest. Female guppies prefer to mate with male guppies that have large bright orange spots on their sides. Meanwhile, predator fish find it easier to catch males with orange spots. So the brightest males are more likely to mate and pass on their genes but are also more likely to get eaten.

The distinctive orange spots of male guppies are preferred by female guppies but also make males easier for predators to see; tradeoffs between attracting mates and avoiding predators are presented as evidence for evolution through natural selection.

The biologists studying these Trinidad guppies were able to do a series of experiments to investigate evolutionary change in just a few years. First, they predicted that without any other influences, the population would evolve to become more orange over time since the males with bright orange spots were expected to have more offspring. Then they captured fish that lived in the sections of the streams low in the mountains where predator fish also lived. The captured fish had small patches of orange but were otherwise dull in color because of the influence of predation. They released this group of fish into pools of the same stream but high in the mountains above waterfalls, which kept predator fish away. A year or so later scientists returned to the release pools to see how the population had changed. The guppies that were living in the ponds were much more orange and brighter than the original fish released. It is important to note that what changed was the population and not the individual fish. The offspring of the released fish varied in the amount of orange they showed. In pools with predators, brightly colored individuals were eaten and left fewer offspring than those that were drab and better camouflaged. However, when there were no predators, the young males with more orange survived and had more offspring than the drab males. Thus, their offspring survived at higher rates, and with each new generation the population became more orange. This simple experiment is strong evidence that evolution by natural selection can occur in a short time span.

WHAT DO YOU THINK?

What kinds of experimental results are most convincing of evolutionary change: laboratory experiments on bacteria or field experiments on fish?

How much change in fossils would convince you that evolution had occurred?

How do you think DNA fingerprinting has affected our confidence in evolution? Which do you find more convincing—seeing change over time or inferring it from DNA?

What kinds of organisms are more likely to be preserved as fossils? Does this influence the study of evolution?

Chapter 3

The eye is a remarkable organ that helps animals see clearly. The shape and structure of the eye is different in many animals, but each tends to have eyes with similar features. Most eyes focus light to help see in low-light conditions. Animal eyes also have pigments, which are sensitive to light, to sense color or movement. Eyes are so complex, in fact, that some people find it impossible to imagine that they could form in small steps over long periods of time. They ask, how could a partial or semifunctional eye be useful, especially if the parts of the eye must work together in interrelated and complex ways? Could the complex parts of an eye have evolved in small steps over long periods of time? Or were the eyes of each animal species created separately rather than coming through a process of evolution?

The complexity of the eye, referred to by some as **irreducible complexity**, is often cited in current criticisms of evolution. Proponents of **intelligent design** argue that structures as complex as the eye could not have arisen in small evolutionary steps and thus can be best explained only through separate creation by an intelligent creator.

Since the days of Darwin, many people have opposed evolution for a variety of scientific and religious reasons. Darwin correctly anticipated that many of the criticisms he would face would be religious in nature.

This closeup of the eye of an elephant shows the complex nature of the mammalian eye, including a retina and cornea.

This famous painting from 1555 by the Italian artist Jacopo Tintoretto shows the biblical view of creation.

The religious opposition to Darwin's ideas was fundamentally based on the idea that the Old Testament of the Bible describes how God created the earth and all the creatures upon it. Man was to reign supreme over all the creatures and the earth. Evolution, according to its critics, dispensed with a creator, demoted humans to simply another type of animal and proposed that species could change. It stood opposed to the idea of a perfect, unchanging creation event. Many of the religious foundations for opposition to evolution persist in present-day creationism, especially in the United States. **Creationism** is the belief that species were created by a supernatural power.

The most common early alternative to evolution is now known as "young-Earth" creationism, which is the belief that life was created by a supernatural being a little over six thousand years ago. Consequently, evolution could not be true because not enough time has passed for evolution to occur. Advances in physics and geology have shown

DID YOU KNOW?

One of the first estimates of the age of the earth came from an Irish Anglican bishop named James Ussher. He estimated the age of each person in the Bible and back-calculated how much time was needed for the biblical events to occur. His estimate was that the earth was formed on October 23, 4004 BCE.

through radioactive dating that the earth is likely much older than six thousand years. Today many of the scientific concerns about the age of the earth have been addressed.

The Creation Museum in Petersburg, Kentucky, presents a young earth creationist view of life; this exhibit shows humans and dinosaurs living at the same time.

Today the two most common alternatives to evolution are progressive creationism and intelligent design. Both are based upon the idea of an intelligent creator, but they differ as to whether new species can form from existing species.

Progressive creationism is the belief that evolutionary processes, such as natural selection, occur within a species but that new species do not form from previous species. Thus, this view rejects the idea of common descent, which by definition proposes that ancestral species gave rise to modern species. Progressive creationism does not dispute estimates of the age of the earth or the fact that populations can change in their characteristics over time owing to natural selection. However, its proponents believe that the fossil record does not show conclusive proof of species changing, and thus modern life cannot be explained by changes over time. Progressive creationism argues that the best explanation for the diversity of life and for **extinction** is the hand of a creator.

Intelligent design holds that some components of organisms could not have evolved in a series of gradual steps because partial structures, such as half an eye, would not be useful. According to this view,

Stages of eye complexity in mollusks

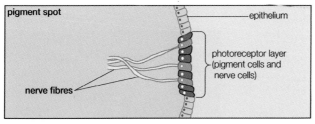

pigment spot

epithelium

photoreceptor layer
(pigment cells and
nerve cells)

nerve fibres

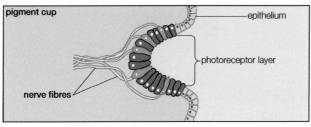

pigment cup

epithelium

photoreceptor layer

nerve fibres

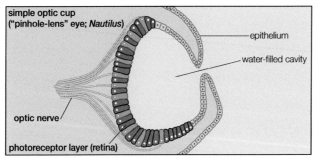

simple optic cup
("pinhole-lens" eye; *Nautilus*)

epithelium

water-filled cavity

optic nerve

photoreceptor layer (retina)

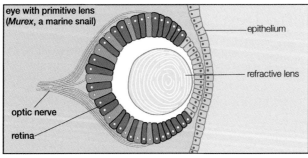

eye with primitive lens
(*Murex*, a marine snail)

epithelium

refractive lens

optic nerve

retina

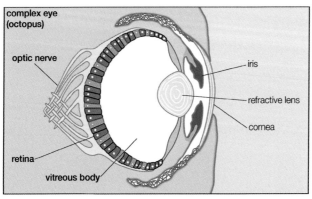

complex eye
(octopus)

optic nerve

iris

refractive lens

cornea

retina

vitreous body

The *Phylum Mollusca*, invertebrates that include octopus, scallops, and snails, show a continium of eye complexity with some species having simple pigmented spots that reveal intensity, intermediate forms that provide information on the direction of light, while others having a complex eye with a cornea and a retina.

a complex feature such as an eye can only be explained as having been created at once and not through a series of evolutionary steps.

Many biologists would join advocates of intelligent design in marveling at the complexity and diversity of life on the earth. However, biologists who study the complex features offered as indications of intelligent design, such as the eye, do not share the view that complexity could not arise through evolution. Instead, they propose the gradations of complexity in the eye observed in modern animals all show a functional response to different conditions. Current research shows that evolution may not always occur in small, slow, even steps over long periods of time but instead may have periods of rapid change that "punctuate" longer periods of equilibrium.

Broader criticism of evolution often focuses on a stated lack of "missing links." According to this argument, if organisms are changing over time, then fossils should show these different stages, called transitional forms. The fact that so few fossils have been found showing a transition from one species to another has been interpreted as evidence against evolution. Biologists counter that fossils are very rare, and so the chances of any one animal or plant being preserved as a fossil is low. Furthermore, with every year, more fossils and transitional forms are discovered.

Evolution and the Language of Science

Science is a process in which criticism and response are integral to the improvement of the understanding of the natural world. Sometimes the specific language and nature of science contribute to confusion about theories. The words "theory," "law," and "fact" all have narrow definitions in science. Each definition is somewhat different from the word's broader use in nonscientific language. Evolution is a **theory**. If evolution is to be believed, why is it not a law?

How does science progress? When hypotheses are tested and supported, they may rise to the level of theory. For a theory to be scientifically valid, it must be possible to test the theory's predictions. If the predictions are not upheld, then the theory must be changed. Scientific knowledge is cumulative—each hypothesis, observation, or theory builds upon those that came before. Experiments and tests show which observations are not repeatable and which hypotheses are good explanations. Ideas are then modified and retested. Only after a long time does a set of explanations rise to become a theory. Criticism and skepticism are important facets of science. At all stages in the scientific process, scientists review each other's hypotheses, data, and conclusions with a skeptical eye. By questioning, critical analysis, and review, scientific knowledge advances.

DID YOU KNOW?

Once it was clear that living organisms were made of cells, geologists began searching for fossils that showed features that looked like cells. Some have estimated that cells might date back more than three billion years.

There is much confusion today about evolution because of a
general misunderstanding of how
scientists use the word theory. In
nonscientific language, a theory
is a best guess, often a speculation without much supporting
evidence. However to scientists, a
theory is just the opposite. A theory
is a well-supported explanation of
an aspect of the natural world. It is
built upon repeatable facts, logic,
and tested and supported hypoth-

Cell theory is the scientific theory that cells are the ba-
sic unit in living organisms; the theory developed over
time through observations and experiments that were
supported through repeated scientific investigations.

eses. Guesses or hunches about how the world works are never considered a scientific theory. In fact, the label "theory" is reserved for ideas
with the strongest level of scientific support. It is used only after many
tests of hypotheses have given the same conclusion. Examples of other
scientific theories are the heliocentric theory (the theory that the earth
revolves around the sun and not vice versa) and the cell theory, which
maintains that all living things are made of building blocks called cells.
Even though both of these theories are now so well-supported that new
observations are unlikely to overturn them, many years ago they began
as controversial hypotheses proposed to explain observations that the
scientific understanding of the time could not.

In addition to theories, science also has laws. However, comparing theories to scientific laws is not appropriate. A scientific law is simply a statement of the results of repeated observation, such as the law of gravity. However, a law does not provide an explanation for the repeated observations. Therefore, it would be inappropriate and impossible to have a law of evolution. Evolution provides an explanation for repeated observations of change in the natural world; therefore it must be a scientific theory.

Additional confusion arises with the word "fact." In science, a fact is a verifiable observation. Like a scientific law, a fact does not provide an explanation for the observations. Only hypotheses and theories explain facts and laws.

Evolution can be considered both a fact and a theory. The facts in this case are scientists' repeatable observations, while the theory is the proposed explanation for the cause of those observations. In the previous chapter, the facts of evolution are that organisms have changed over time, as revealed in the fossil record and in experiments, such as that with the Trinidad guppies. The theory is the proposed cause of the documented change. In this case, the proposed theory is that of descent with modification, meaning organisms have diverged from common ancestors through natural selection and other evolutionary forces.

Who Opposes Evolution?

Recent surveys of biologists, scientists that study life, found that more than 99 percent thought that the theory of evolution best explained modern living organisms. Some scientists oppose evolution, but the most vocal scientists who criticize evolution are not trained in biology. Even though these scientists have advanced degrees in difficult fields such as chemistry and physics, they usually do not have training and experience to evaluate the evidence for evolution. In other words, the group of scientists best trained to evaluate the evidence for evolution overwhelmingly supports the theory.

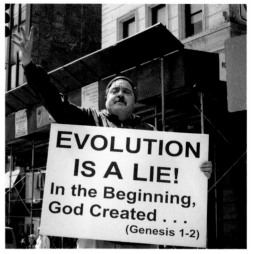

Opposition to the modern theory of evolution is widespread; statistics show that more than 39% of Americans surveyed opposed evolution, with Turkey the only nation in the world having a higher percentage of opposition.

Excluding biologists, a significant number of U.S. citizens question the validity of evolution as an explanation for life on earth. The number of people who oppose evolution in other countries is much lower. The reasons for this opposition are varied and complicated. For many people, the potential implications of the shared ancestry of life are troubling and contradict a faith-based belief system.

Is There Confidence in Modern Biology?

One central idea of how science works is that knowledge is tentative and always subject to be shown to be false. Thus, the theory of evolution is not set in stone. Our understanding of how evolution works has changed since Darwin, so it is best to focus disagreements on modern ideas and not those proposed over 150 years ago. For example,

THE SCOPES MONKEY TRIAL

The famous court case sometimes called the Scopes Monkey Trial took place in 1925 in Dayton, Tennessee. A teacher, John Scopes, was on trial for teaching evolution to his high school biology students. Because of public opinion, the trial became a big event. Two famous lawyers battled over whether Scopes had broken the law. So many people came to listen that the judge often held court outdoors under a large tree. Scopes was found guilty of violating a state law that prohibited teaching evolution. Much later in time, the U.S. Supreme Court ruled that state laws prohibiting the teaching of evolution violated the Constitution.

John Scopes (1900-1970) deliberately violated Tennessee's law against teaching evolution in order to draw attention to what he viewed as an unjust law.

we now understand that natural selection is not the only force driving evolution, an idea that Darwin did not propose. Random changes in genetic material, termed **genetic drift**, and isolation of populations are also critical evolutionary forces. In the same way that Albert Einstein's theory of relativity altered Sir Isaac Newton's conception of physics considerably, it is possible that new discoveries will fundamentally alter our understanding of evolution. Therefore, evolutionary biology is a tentative science that evolves itself as evidence changes our understanding. Evolutionary biologists must be open to evidence that could contradict aspects of evolutionary theory. In the same way, creationists should be willing to evaluate evidence independent of the implications of the conclusions it leads to. Only then will we be able to engage in an open respectful debate about life on the earth.

WHAT DO YOU THINK?

If an eye had only some of its parts, could it still help focus light and help with vision?

Why do you think opposition to evolutionary biology changed over time? Which arguments are most convincing to you?

How do you use the word theory? Does calling something a theory suggest it is well thought out or simply a speculation?

How much evidence do you think there is for new species forming from older species?

Do you think the Bible is a text that should play a role in science— for example, in determining the age of the earth? What do you think is the best evidence for determining the age of the earth?

Chapter 4

How can you decide whether to accept or reject the main-stream scientific theory of evolution? Fundamentally, evolution is about changes over time and does not directly address the special status of humans. Evolution can be simply defined as change in a population of organisms over time. This makes it possible for you to evaluate specific cases and decide for yourself whether evolutionary change best explains observed patterns.

Evolution and Everyday Life

For much of human history, being infected by a pathogen often meant death. In the late 1800s, Louis Pasteur and other scientists isolated and produced powerful drugs that could kill a bacterial infection. These drugs were called antibiotics, and since then their use has become widespread in modern medicine and in raising livestock. One unexpected consequence of frequent antibiotic use is that bacteria acquire resistance to the common drugs used to fight infections. The process begins when a small number of bacteria survive the antibiotic because of changes in their genetic information. After most of the other bacteria are killed, the small number of individuals with resistance grow and

The performance of middle and high school students in the U.S. has declined over the last thirty years compared to performance in Asia and Europe.

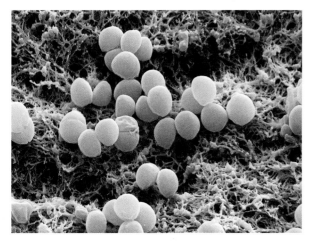

MRSA is a strain of the bacterium Staphylococcus that is resistant to many forms of antibiotics and is an increasing infectious agent in difficult to treat infections.

form the next generation. As this process repeats itself, the resistance of each group of bacteria to an antibiotic drug increases.

Thus, we have unwittingly conducted our own experiment by creating strong natural selection for antibiotic resistance. Historically, U.S. medical doctors automatically prescribed antibiotics to patients. In Europe and many other countries, doctors used antibiotics only if infections would not clear up on their own. One consequence of this difference in practice is higher levels of antibiotic resistance in the United States than in Europe. Many strains of bacteria, especially in hospitals, have become resistant to all modern antibiotics. To become infected often means to die. One cause of increased resistance is the inappropriate prescription of antibiotics when patients do not actually have bacterial infections. Also, patients frequently do not follow instructions and continue to take their medicine after symptoms subside.

Imagine that you are a parent with a sick child. Your son has been running a very high fever. The doctor tells you that a virus is causing your son's fever. You ask if your son should have antibiotics. The doctor says no and explains that antibiotics do not have any effect on viruses, only on bacteria.

WHAT DO YOU THINK?

> **Should our approach to public health consider the evolutionary implications of prescribing antibiotics?**

> **Should the media be encouraged to use the word "evolution" when describing antibiotic resistance rather than the term "develop" in order to help people understand why the problem is occurring?**

> **How can people be encouraged to continue taking prescribed antibiotics to help avoid antibiotic resistance evolving?**

Evolution and Conservation

Defining a species is not just a question for science. The Endangered Species Act (1973) is a landmark conservation law that authorizes the U.S. government to take action to avoid the extinction of native animals and plants. To follow the law, it is necessary to define a group of individuals as a distinct species; that is, a group with a shared and distinct evolutionary history. Scientists and wildlife managers must detect which groups are distinct enough to protect.

One interesting case study of potential conflict concerns the wolves that are found in the northern Great Lakes region, in the states of Minnesota, Michigan, and Wisconsin, as well as in Canada. Because of overhunting, the original population of wolves found in the region was reduced to only a small number of individuals. However, following protection from the U.S. government, the wolf population has grown to over four thousand. The government is planning to remove the wolves

The gray wolf, *Canis lupus*, is the largest member of the dog family and forms packs that range across large areas of forest and grassland.

from the protection of the Endangered Species Act because it believes they have recovered.

Recently, scientists collected blood and tissue from living wolves and from specimens in museums to test whether the wolves that live in the Great Lakes region right now are the same species as the wolves that lived there prior to hunting. When they compared the DNA, the results were surprising. They found that prior to overhunting, the group of animals that lived in the Great Lakes area was a distinct species—a species more closely related to coyotes than to wolves. Although the animals looked like wolves, they shared more in common genetically with coyotes. The modern animals are a mix of genetic material from this original population, western wolves, and eastern coyotes. Some people propose that this new information indicates that this group of wolves is distinct and requires continued government protection from hunting.

WHAT DO YOU THINK?

Should a distinct evolutionary history entitle a group of organisms to protection from extinction? For example, if wolves are common in Montana, do we need to protect wolves that are endangered in Michigan?

What should the government do in this case? Remove protection and let people hunt wolves with the required permits? Or continue to protect this distinct population of animals?

Evolution and Modern Medicine

The quality of human life has been greatly increased by the clinical and research work done by physicians. However, because medicine is focused on the immediate causes of disease to determine treatment, it may sometimes benefit from considering how evolution has shaped humans and their chances of getting sick. In the same way, evolutionary biologists rarely consider the human health applications of their findings. Recently, a new field has emerged called evolutionary medicine, which combines the study of medicine and evolutionary biology.

One important finding has been how evolutionary history has influenced humans. Doing one thing well means doing another thing less well. Take as an example the acidity of the human stomach. The strong acid environment in the stomach keeps most bacteria from growing and thus prevents infection. However, acid levels just higher than the norm can cause stomach ulcers, suggesting a delicate balance between too much and too little acid. Seeing the integration between these two factors can help a medical doctor understand the balance that has evolved over time. Another example of evolutionary applications to medicine is obesity. In the past, foods such as sugar and fat were scarce. Humans likely evolved the behavior of craving these scarce and energy-dense foods. In modern life sugary and fatty foods are inexpensive and common, but we still crave them and eat them at levels that can greatly reduce our health. An evolutionary perspective can help explain why we act in ways that might eventually harm us.

Many scientists have argued that evolution should be a required course in medical training, either before attending medical school or during training as physicians. Others have argued that evolution is not important to modern medicine or that its importance is too limited to require training.

WHAT DO YOU THINK?

How much of the human body can be explained by the evolutionary past?

Do you think understanding evolution is important for medical doctors?

Can you think of other aspects of human behavior and physiology that might reveal an evolutionary influence on health?

Evolution in Public Schools

Many people, particularly those with strong religious views, oppose the central ideas of evolutionary biology. They believe that teaching evolution in the classroom may lead young children to lose their faith. In the recent past in Texas and some other states, information concerning evolution was removed from textbooks. Because this action was ruled unconstitutional, it was overruled by a federal appeals court.

In contrast to most states, the Texas State Board of Education chooses textbooks for every school district in the state, thus giving it a lot of power and public attention.

As a response, it is common to attempt to place stickers in textbooks alerting students to evolution being "just a theory." In other locations, teachers who are skeptical of evolution have chosen to teach progressive creationism or intelligent design in the classroom. Parents, concerned about the "separation of church and state," have complained.

WHAT DO YOU THINK?

Do you think that instructors teaching evolution need to highlight that it is just a theory and not a law or a fact? How does a misunderstanding of scientific theories affect whether textbook warnings are a good idea?

Should communities keep public schools from teaching evolution?

Should evolution and its alternatives be taught in the classroom? What are the benefits of presenting multiple ideas?

Do you think the alternatives to evolution are religious or scientific in nature?

Glossary

artificial selection—Purposeful selection by humans to change one or more features of a plant or animal.

creationism—The doctrine or theory holding that species were created by a supernatural being.

descent with modification—Darwin's central idea that organisms share traits in common because they inherited them from a common ancestor and that over time these traits change owing to natural selection.

DNA—The genetic material that provides the blueprint for making cells and is passed from one generation to the next.

Enlightenment—A philosophical movement starting in 1650 that sought to use reason to reform understanding of the world.

extinction—The disappearance of a species.

fossil—The preserved remains of species that lived in the past.

genetic drift—changes in genetic information that occur through chance events and not through influences on survival and reproduction.

hypothesis—A proposed explanation for a pattern or phenomenon.

intelligent design—The belief that certain features of life are best explained by an intelligent designer rather than through natural causes.

irreducible complexity—The characteristic of a biological structure that is deemed too complex to have evolved from a simpler structure.

mutation—A change in genetic material.

naturalist—An individual who studies plants and animals.

natural selection—A natural process whereby a population changes over time in its composition owing to certain individuals having better features for survival and reproduction in a particular environment.

ornithological—Relating to the study of birds.

pollinator—any organism that transfer pollen from one plant individual to another.

species—A group of organisms that share a common recent evolutionary history.

theory—A body of principles supported through repeated observations and experiments that explain a phenomenon.

trait—Any definable feature of an organism.

vertebrate—a group of animals that have vertebratal columns; includes fish, amphibians, reptiles, birds, and mammals.

vestigial—Characteristic of an existing bodily part or organ that no longer appears to have a function.

Find Out More

Books

Coyne, Jerry A. *Why Evolution Is True*. New York: Penguin, 2010.

Dembski, William, and Sean McDowell. *Understanding Intelligent Design: Everything You Need to Know in Plain Language*. Eugene, OR: Harvest House, 2008.

Lawson, Kristan. *Darwin and Evolution for Kids: His Life and Ideas with 21 Activities*. Chicago: Chicago Review Press, 2003.

Science, Evolution, and Creationism. 2008. Committee on Revising Science and Creationism: A View from the National Academy of Sciences, National Academy of Sciences and Institute of Medicine of the National Academies. Free download from nap.edu.

Websites

The Talk Origins Archive
www.talkorigins.org

Discovery Institute
http://www.discovery.org

Understanding Evolution
http://evolution.berkeley.edu

Institute for Creation Research
http://www.icr.org

Index

Page numbers in boldface are illustrations.

About the Authors

Dan Ardia, a biology professor, teaches evolution and studies the evolution of bird behavior. He received a Ph. D. in ecology and evolutionary biology from Cornell University in 2004. He enjoys world travel, basketball, and playing with his children outdoors.

Elizabeth Rice is an adjunct professor of biology. She earned her doctorate from Cornell University while studying corn genetics and conservation of genetic diversity in Mexico. She enjoys gardening, hiking, cooking, sewing, and following her two small children on their adventures.